TABLE OF CONTENTS

Chapter 1: Introduction

On September 11, 2001, 19 terrorists belonging to the militant Islamic organization Al Qaeda killed over 3000 American citizens by hijacking airplanes and flying them into the World Trade Center in New York City and the Pentagon in Washington D.C. A fourth plane heading for Washington D.C. crashed in a field in Pennsylvania when the passengers fought back against the terrorists. Like the Japanese attack on Pearl Harbor the morning of December 7, 1941, or the sinking of the USS Maine in Havana, Cuba the night of February 15, 1898, Al Qaeda's surprise attack galvanized the nation and was the catalyst that took a peaceful nation into war.

In response to the September 11th attacks, the United States initiated an aggressive campaign to defeat the Al Qaeda terrorist organization. A few short months later, during Operation Enduring Freedom, the United States overthrew the Taliban regime in Afghanistan, preventing that country from being used as a base of operations for Al Qaeda and forcing the organization's leadership into hiding. Unfortunately, the fall of the Taliban did not spell the end of Al Qaeda. The organization has demonstrated remarkable resiliency and survivability. Al Qaeda has adapted to the new environment and established a complex and adaptive web of physical, social, legal, and virtual sanctuaries through which they obtain necessary resources and control their operations worldwide.

Intelligence estimates suggest that Al Qaeda has relocated its leadership and training camps to the Northwest Frontier Provinces of Pakistan[1]—a tribal area in which the local Pashtu

---

[1] Bill Roggio, "Al Qaeda's Pakistan Sanctuary: Musharraf Appeases the Taliban." *The Weekly Standard*, Volume 12, Issue 28 (April 2007),

people are sympathetic to Al Qaeda's anti-Western views and where the government of Pakistan has little political or physical control. Within the sovereign borders of Pakistan, Al Qaeda remains sheltered from U.S. military and political power.

This physical refuge provides Al Qaeda freedom of action to leverage modern technology to conduct their information operations and to communicate with their followers and sympathizers around the world. Al Qaeda's use of the open internet with its capability to easily and quickly transmit audio and video messages, combined with other electronic communications such as global 24-hour news television, cell phone messaging and video sharing, and even old-fashioned shortwave radio broadcasts, have provided Al Qaeda with a form of "virtual sanctuary" that has proven extremely effective. Senior leaders of Al-Qaeda have sent videotaped messages to media outlets that many intelligence analysts believe contain coded messages to geographically-separated operational cells, other related insurgent groups, and supporting organizations providing finances, logistics, membership, and transportation.[2] Recently, Ayman al-Zawahiri, the organization's second-in-command, offered to answer written questions submitted by "individuals, agencies, and all media"[3] via web forums operated by Al Qaeda's media arm, As Sahab. From the virtual sanctuary of the worldwide web, As Sahab has

---

http://www.weeklystandard.com/Content/Public/Articles/000/000/013/457rzpvh.asp (Accessed March 5, 2008).

[2] Timothy L. Thomas, *Cyber Silhouettes: Shadows Over Information Operations* (Fort Leavenworth: Foreign Military Studies Office, 2005), 33.

[3] The Associated Press, "Al Qaeda: We're Open to Questions," *CNN.com/world* (December 19, 2007) http://edition.cnn.com/2007/WORLD/meast/12/19/alqaeda.interview.ap/. Accessed December 21, 2007.

established websites through which they can communicate anonymously to deliver training and motivational videos and other propaganda to members, cells, and recruits, and to control operations.

Al Qaeda's actions are further enabled by operating under the protection of the laws and freedoms of the western democracies they seek to destroy. This astute use of "legal sanctuary" is ironic. Many of Al Qaeda's websites operate from servers located in the United States or other western countries where civil liberties make it difficult for the law enforcement and intelligence agencies to monitor or disrupt Al Qaeda's communications. As demonstrated by the September 11th hijackers, Al Qaeda operatives infiltrated western countries in order to obtain training, funding, and a myriad of other resources. The hijackers legally entered the United States on student visas to obtain flight training in the United States. As they had no prior criminal records, the US legal system protected their rights to travel, congregate, study, and say what they wished. They used the legal sanctuary of US law for terrorist gains.

Terrorist organizations have also used legal sanctuary to secure resources. In 1996, a routine investigation into cigarette smuggling in North Carolina led to a multi-year Federal Bureau of Investigation (FBI) investigation revealing a large scale funding operation for the Lebanese terrorist organization Hezbollah. Several Lebanese citizens obtained U.S. citizenship through marriage. They then formed a cell that smuggled millions of dollars worth of cigarettes from North Carolina, a state with low taxes on cigarettes, to Michigan where the taxes are much higher and sent the profits to Hezbollah.[4] The fact that Hezbollah was operating within US borders demonstrates a dilemma western democracies face when dealing with terrorists—should they be treated as criminals and thus subject to the same rights and legal protections as regular citizens, or do the terrorists require a different set of rules? The question of sanctuary, in its legal, physical, and virtual forms must be addressed as the nation adjusts to the evolving threats posed by trans-national, radical, Islamist insurgent groups wishing to impose their values and ideals upon western democracies.

The Oxford English dictionary defines sanctuary as "a place of refuge or safety."[5] The term refuge suggests the first component of sanctuary: protection from danger or hardship. The requirement for protection stems from a mismatch in the relative strengths and capabilities between two opponents. Throughout history, weaker armies have used asymmetric tactics to fight larger, stronger armies. This asymmetry in capabilities forces the weaker opponent to employ non-traditional methods and strategies that avoid the strengths and exploit the weaknesses of the stronger opponent[6]. Traditionally this has meant avoiding decisive battle against a larger and better-equipped army in favor of indirect attacks against the enemy's populace, governmental agencies, financial institutions, or other "soft" targets. In its simplest form, asymmetric warfare may be defined as a "conflict in which the two sides have different weapons available to them

---

[4] http://www.tkb.org/CaseHome.jsp?caseid=615, accessed December 21, 2007.

[5] http://www.askoxford.com/concise_oed/sanctuary?view=uk, accessed April 15, 2008.

[6] For clarity and simplicity the term Insurgent will be used from this point to denote the weaker opponent and the term Counterinsurgent will be used for the stronger opponent.

and pursue different strategies."[7] This disparity in relative strength forces the weaker opponent to seek sanctuary in order to preserve and protect his resources from the stronger foe.

In recent history, a common form of asymmetric warfare has been insurgency. JP 1-02, *Department of Defense Dictionary of Military and Associated Terms*, defines an insurgency as "an organized movement aimed at the overthrow of a constituted government through the use of subversion and armed conflict."[8] During the eighteenth, nineteenth, and twentieth centuries the colonial era came to a turbulent end. Fueled by the Enlightenment and propelled by the American and French revolutions, many colonized nations demanded national independence, social equality, and democratic reforms. In many cases, this led to armed insurrections. Unable to defeat the stronger colonizing armies upon the battlefield, the indigenous populations resorted to insurgent tactics and mobilization of the populace to fight their wars of independence.

The frequency and efficacy of insurgent warfare resulted in considerable publication of writings, theories, and doctrines regarding insurgency. In most cases both insurgents and counterinsurgents identified some form of refuge as a critical component of an insurgency. Various writers refer to sanctuary as a base area, a safe haven, or a sanctuary. Without sanctuaries, insurgencies are vulnerable to counterinsurgent forces. Thus, sanctuary provides a safe haven from which the insurgent can marshal resources against the stronger foe. Sanctuary

---

[7] Coral Bell, "Asymmetric Wars," *Asymmetry and Complexity: Selected papers from the 2005 Rowell Seminar and the 2005 Chief of Army's Conference*, ed. Scott Hopkins (Canberra: Land Warfare Studies Institute, 2007), 5.

[8] JP1-02, *Department of Defense Dictionary of Military and Associated Terms*, April 12, 2001 (as amended through March 4, 2008), 267.

also provides refuge to conduct training and control the activities of insurgent elements. Insurgency expert Bernard Fall defined sanctuary as "a territory contiguous to a rebellious area which, though ostensibly not involved in the conflict, provides the rebel side with shelter, training facilities, equipment, and—if it can get away with it—troops."[9] This definition lacks the component of protection from counterinsurgent forces, but highlights the second key component of sanctuary as it relates to insurgency, access to or provision of resources to the insurgent. For the purpose of this monograph we will define sanctuary as refuge comprised of various modalities which provides insurgent forces both access to critical resources and protection from counterinsurgent efforts.

Historically, physical sanctuary has been the most common form used by insurgents and, as a result, the preponderance of studies analyzing the role of sanctuary deal primarily with physical sanctuary. Technological advancements and the increasing capabilities of non-state actors, however, have resulted in a more complex environment in which insurgents may leverage not only physical, but social, legal and virtual sanctuaries. Modern, global, non-state insurgents such as Al Qaeda and its affiliates do so with great effect. Together, these various forms of sanctuary serve as nodes within a complex and adaptive system. The more forms of sanctuary an insurgency combines, the more well-buffered their system. Targeting only one type of sanctuary is largely ineffective--as soon as you defeat one mode of sanctuary, the successful insurgent leverages another mode.

----

[9] Bernard B. Fall, *Street Without Joy*, (New York: Schocken Books, 1972),375.

This paper will demonstrate that in order to successfully defeat a complex and adaptive web of sanctuary, operational planners must first develop a holistic understanding of the insurgent's system of sanctuaries. Only through an informed understanding of the insurgent's system of sanctuaries can planners apply feasible, appropriate and synchronized effects across the broad spectrum of sanctuary. In short, planners must understand and frame the problem before they can develop solutions.

The question this paper will examine is, "Is current US joint military doctrine adequate for dealing with complex and adaptive systems?" In addition, the study will determine if doctrine provides operational planners the flexibility and cognitive tools to adapt to the amorphous, non-kinetic environment that is an insurgency; the US military's recent experience in the Global War on Terror (GWOT) suggests that the doctrine does not. Five years after toppling the Taliban regime and expelling Al Qaeda from Afghanistan, the Taliban are still conducting an insurgency to combat the newly established Afghan government and the US and NATO presence there. From their sanctuary in Pakistan, Al Qaeda's senior leaders remain alive and continue to direct terrorist activities worldwide. In Iraq, the US military also faces an insurgency which successfully leverages sanctuary.

Outdated counterinsurgency doctrine played a role in the US military's inability to deny the enemy sanctuary in Afghanistan and Iraq. A new US manual prescribing counterinsurgency doctrine was not published until 2006, in response to the wars in Afghanistan and Iraq. The lack of new and updated counterinsurgent doctrine at the beginning of Operations Enduring Freedom and Iraqi Freedom forced the US military to rely upon theories that predate modern forms of media and globalization. As a result, when faced with insurgencies in Iraq and Afghanistan, the US focused largely on physical sanctuary and failed to account for sanctuary's other forms.

As the paper analyzes the various modalities of sanctuary in an insurgency, it will discuss how these forms of sanctuary comprise a complex adaptive system, and apply the emerging concept of Commander's Appreciation and Campaign Design (CACD) as a useful analytical tool for planners to understand problems and design operations against insurgent sanctuary. This paper will first discuss the roots of sanctuary in modern insurgent warfare and explore the various types of sanctuary. In chapter 2, a discussion of complex adaptive systems and the complex adaptive nature of sanctuary will lay the theoretical framework for the study. Finally, a discussion of CACD will explain its principles and demonstrate its utility in dealing with complexity and adaptation. Throughout, the paper will use case studies to illustrate the salient points.

Chapter 2: The Roots of Sanctuary in Modern Insurgent Warfare

As an armed struggle to overthrow a constituted government through subversion and armed conflict, insurgencies seek to establish themselves as the legitimate government of the concerned populace. As such, winning the "hearts and minds" of the people determines victory in an insurgency. The side with the most appealing ideology and the ability to impose that ideology will carry the day. For the insurgent, as long as he can sustain his ideology and means to propagate it, the insurgency remains a threat to the established government. By providing refuge from counterinsurgent actions and access to resources, sanctuary ensures the survivability of the insurgent's ideology and capabilities, and is, therefore, a vital component of an insurgency.

Despite the frequency of asymmetric wars during the post-colonial era, until recently US military doctrine remained fixated on fighting conventional wars against peer or near-peer foes. As a result, current US counterinsurgency doctrine relied heavily upon the recorded lessons learned by both insurgents and counterinsurgents during the last half of the twentieth century—a body of literature which largely predates modern forms of information technology and globalization. Though the literature clearly acknowledges the important role of sanctuary in an insurgency, the focus is predominantly upon the roles of physical, or geographic, sanctuary and social sanctuary. Modern information technology and rapid globalization, however, have lead to newer and more advanced forms of sanctuary. Collectively these forms of sanctuary reinforce an insurgency's ability to keep its ideology alive.

Sanctuary in Insurgency Doctrine: Mao Zedong and Ho Chi Minh

The writings of Mao Zedong remain perhaps the most influential theory regarding the conduct of an insurgency. As the leader of the Chinese Communist party, Mao waged an insurgency against the Chinese Nationalist government during the first half of the twentieth century. Initially lacking the military means to challenge the stronger, US backed, Nationalist forces, Mao developed a powerful rural insurgency that eschewed a decisive battle of annihilation in favor of a strategy of exhaustion. This required a long-term strategy in which the Communists politicized and mobilized the rural populace to provide resources with which to form an army. In order to do this, the Communists required the freedom of maneuver afforded by both physical sanctuary and popular support.[10]

In *The Struggle in the Chinkang Mountains*, written November 1928, Mao identifies a "sound mass base" and "economic resources sufficient for sustenance" as elements critical to the survival and growth of his insurgent movement.[11] In his treatise *Problems of Strategy in Guerilla War Against Japan*, written in 1938, Mao discussed the concept of base areas. Mao stated that the establishment of base areas is a fundamental principle "to be adopted before we can attain the object of preserving and expanding ourselves and destroying the enemy," and that "it will be

---

[10] Paret, *Makers of Modern Strategy: from Machiavelli to the Nuclear Age*, (Princeton: Princeton University Press, 1986), 839.

impossible to sustain guerilla warfare behind enemy lines without base areas."[12] Mao then

categorized these base areas into three geographic types: mountains, plains, and river-lake-estuary

regions. This focus on physical sanctuary is understandable as Chinese Communists had few

resources to work with except the refuge and bounty provided by the rugged mountainous terrain.

During Mao's struggles against the Nationalist Chinese, as well as the Japanese armies, the

Communist forces continually relied upon the sanctuary of China's mountains as base areas.

Within these physical sanctuaries, they mobilized the populace to provide food, create and repair

equipment, and provide manpower.

The mountains also provided a physical barrier that protected the Communists from their

enemies. The Nationalist forces used conventional tactics that required large formations of troops

and were bound to roads as their primary lines of communication back to bases in the urban areas.

The large troop formations used by the Nationalists required significant logistical support. In the

rugged terrain of the mountains, narrow roads were easily interdicted by small numbers of

guerrillas, requiring more Nationalist forces just to secure the tenuous supply lines. Facing the

prospect of committing, and possibly losing, significant resources just to defeat a handful of

guerillas forced the Nationalists to concede significant geographic regions to the Communists.

---

[11]Mao Zedong, *Selected Military Writings of Mao Tse Tung*, (Fort Leavenworth: Combat Studies Institute), 21.

[12] Ibid, 167. Mao defines base areas as "strategic bases on which guerilla forces rely in performing their strategic tasks and achieving the object of preserving and expanding themselves and destroying or driving out the enemy."

The terrain provided the Communist forces both a significant refuge from the Nationalist forces as well as valuable and necessary resources.

The Vietnamese leaders Ho Chi Minh and Vo Nguyen Giap were heavily influenced by the example and writings of Mao during their struggle to obtain independence from first the Japanese, then the French, and the Americans. Ho and Giap capitalized upon physical and social sanctuary in Vietnam then leveraged information and world opinion as a crude form of virtual sanctuary. In response to the Japanese occupation of the northern Tonkin region of Vietnam in 1940, Ho and Giap organized propaganda teams and prepared articles, pamphlets, and banners advocating a general uprising to obtain liberation.[13] During the wars against the Japanese and French, Ho and Giap used information primarily to encourage support for their cause by the Vietnamese population. During the war against the Americans, Ho expanded his information operations to a wider audience by using the US and international news organizations to influence world opinion in his favor.[14]

Sanctuary in Counterinsurgency Doctrine

In addition to Vietnam, Mao's model of revolutionary warfare heavily influenced numerous other insurgencies worldwide in the last half of the twentieth century. Armies trained and equipped to fight the conventional battles during the two World Wars struggled to adapt to

---

[13] John Shy and Collier, "Revolutionary Warfare," *Makers of Modern Strategy: from Machiavelli to the Nuclear Age*, ed. Peter Paret, (Princeton: Princeton University. Press, 1986), 846-847

[14] Ho Chi Minh, O*n Revolution: Selected Writings, 1920-66*, ed. Bernard B. Fall, (New York: Frederick A. Praeger Publishers, 1967), this book contains numerous letters written by Ho Chi Minh to various western press agencies and governments. .

counterinsurgency warfare. The British army faced Mao-inspired Communist insurgencies in Malaya, Cypress and Kenya and the French fought against insurgencies in Algeria and Indochina, just to name a few. This resulted in a wealth of counterinsurgency study and doctrine which acknowledged the role of sanctuary and identified gaining the support of the local populace as the most effective means of denying sanctuary to the insurgent.

David Galula, a French military officer with considerable counterinsurgency experience garnered from assignments in China, Greece and Algeria from 1945 until 1958 published the book *Counterinsurgency Warfare: Theory and Practice* in 1964. In defining the characteristics of a successful insurgency, Galula cited the significance of physical sanctuary stating that, "By moving from one side of the border to the other, the insurgent is often able to escape pressure or, at least, to complicate operations for his opponent."[15] Galula also suggested that during the early stages of an insurgency, insurgents must operate in remote areas far from the center of the counterinsurgent's power, preferably on both sides of administrative borders to make it difficult for a coordinated counterinsurgent reaction.[16] Though Galula was principally speaking about geographic refuge, the concept of isolation and refuge from counterinsurgent reaction is valid for other modalities of counterinsurgent reaction. Exploiting seams in laws or the anonymity of modern information technology can provide insurgents with refuge from the counterinsurgents.

---

[15] David Galula, *Counterinsurgency Warfare: Theory and Practice*, (New York: Frederick A. Praeger Publishers, 1964), 35

[16] Ibid, 51.

Also writing in the 1960s, British Colonel Julian Paget analyzed the insurgencies in Malaya, Kenya, and Cypress to distill five basic requirements for a successful insurgency: a cause, support from the local populace, bases, mobility, and supplies. In discussing the requirement for bases he stated, "The ideal position for the guerillas is to be in possession not only of secure bases, but also of an inviolate 'sanctuary', accessible to them, but not to the security [counterinsurgent] forces."[17]

Both Galula and Paget acknowledged the difficulty in countering sanctuary. Discussing the challenge of combating physical sanctuary, Galula stated that, "Geographic factors...cannot be significantly changed or influenced except by displacing the population...or by building artificial fences."[18] Paget suggested that "operations against the insurgent bases depend on good intelligence if they are to be effective."[19] In regards to bases that take advantage of political boundaries, he suggested that special political action will be required, as well as cooperation from law enforcement agencies and other branches of the military.[20]

Forms of Sanctuary in Insurgency

A theme common to all studies of insurgency, both insurgent and counterinsurgent, is the primacy of social factors. Insurgents fight to wrest the support of the populace away from the

---

[17] Julian Paget, *Counter-Insurgency Operations: Techniques of Guerilla Warfare*, (New York: Walker and Company, 1967), 25.

[18] Galula, *Counterinsurgency Warfare*, 67.

[19] Paget, *Counter-Insurgency Operations*, 170.

[20] Ibid, 171.

counterinsurgent government. In his study of insurgency *War of the Flea*, Robert Taber said, "Without the consent and active aid of the people, the guerilla would be merely a bandit, and could not long survive."[21] It follows, then, that physical sanctuary, in and of itself, possesses no intrinsic value. Rather, its efficacy is inextricably linked to societal conditions. Changes in society have led to changes in the concept of sanctuary. As a result, insurgents can leverage multiple forms of sanctuary beyond simple physical, geographic refuge

Physical and Social Sanctuary

Physical sanctuary is the most common form of sanctuary as it is the least complex--it requires only terrain. Physical sanctuary is the geographic base area as described by Mao and may be defined as geographic regions which provide insurgents access to resources and protection from counterinsurgent influence, most often provided by restrictive terrain, political borders, or logistical constraints which prevent access to the counterinsurgent.

Social sanctuary is the refuge and access to resources provided by societal factors. It is most often afforded to insurgents by people sympathetic to the insurgent cause, usually as a result of common social factors such as ethnicity, tribal affiliation, religion, political beliefs, or shared heritage.

---

[21] Robert Taber, *War of the Flea: the Classic Study of Guerrilla Warfare*, (Washington D.C.: Brassey's Inc, 2002), 12.

The Chinese Communists leveraged popular support as an effective form of social sanctuary. The Chinese Communist revolt originated as a response to the feudal system still in place at the beginning of the twentieth century. The Communist party's proposed socialist reforms were an attractive alternative. Mao acknowledged that, "The richest source of power to wage war lies in the masses of the people."[22] As such, he admonished Communist soldiers not to alienate the populace through brigandry; advocating, instead, unity between the army and the people through respect and enthusiastic political mobilization. As Communist forces gained control of areas, they implemented land reforms, confiscating land from the wealthy and redistributing it throughout the population. They also established regional political cadre to recruit and indoctrinate the population. [23] These methods to gain popular support strengthened the Communist base areas by providing willing manpower, food and other resources. When Communist forces defeated National forces, they offered their defeated foe clemency and employment. In addition to manpower and weapons, this tactic provided them information and intelligence as Nationalist soldiers switched allegiance in considerable numbers.

Mao's dictums regarding the conduct of his Communists soldiers among the populace illustrate the importance he placed on the social aspect of sanctuary. When combined, physical and social sanctuary form a formidable system. The synergy of physical and social factors contributing to the Communist's sanctuary also suggests the complex nature of sanctuary. The efficacy of the Communist geographic base areas was greatly enhanced by the social conditions.

---

[22] Mao, *Selected Writings*, 260.

[23] Ibid, 35.

The actions of sympathetic peasants and converted Nationalist soldiers helped provide refuge from Nationalist forces and critical resources to the Communists.

The experience of the Chinese Communists was most certainly not the first example of weaker opponents seeking geographic and social refuge from stronger opponents. At the turn of the nineteenth century, Napoleon's Grand Armee reigned supreme in Europe. In 1808, Napoleon seized Spain, beginning a six-year-long occupation during which the French army faced persistent resistance from Spanish guerillas. Despite maintaining over 250,000 troops in Spain through 1812, the French army was unable to mass against the elusive Spanish resistance while guarding its long lines of communication through the rugged mountainous terrain of the Navarre, Aragon and Basque provinces of Spain.[24] Furthermore, the mountains served as ideal physical sanctuary for Spanish guerrillas as they provided shelter from French forces and access to critical resources. The French combined arms tactics using infantry, artillery and cavalry were poorly suited for the rugged confines of Spain's mountains. The terrain was impassable to French artillery and cavalry, prevented the employment of massed formations of infantry, and left dangerously exposed lines of communication back to French bases in the plains and urban areas.

The Spanish mountains also provided sufficient resources for the insurgents. The mountains' ample annual rainfall and mild weather ensured adequate agricultural productivity to sustain a large guerilla force. Farmers in the mountains could grow two crops per year, whereas farmers on the plains could only grow one. Without ready access to large markets, the mountain communities produced a wider variety of crops and kept more livestock than the urban communities.[25] Each of these factors made the mountain villages more self-sufficient than the towns in the lowlands.

Social conditions in the mountains also contributed to the French inability to deny the sanctuary provided to the Spanish guerrillas. A long history of political and economic egalitarianism and independence heavily contributed to the efficacy of the mountains as a sanctuary. The Navarre region was one of the few in Spain that maintained its own ancient constitution, or *fuero*, dating back to the Middle Ages.[26] Under this traditional agreement, in return for limited interference by the Spanish monarch the people of the Navarre agreed to contribute people and funds for war against invaders. The *fuero* also allowed the people of the Navarre to maintain their own executive and legislative bodies. The regional Congress, the *Cortes*, was comprised of ecclesiastics, nobles, and commoners. This ensured a balance of power among the three major social castes in the region and gave each a sense of ownership for and responsibility to the system. This unique system contributed to the low social stratification in the society.

The low social stratification was also a function of the concept of nobility in the region. In the Navarre, nobility was considered to belong inalienably to all native inhabitants.[27] Impervious to past foreign invaders, the population in the mountainous regions of Spain

---

[24] John L. Tone, *The Fatal Knot*, (Chapel Hill: The University of North Carolina Press, 1994), 4.

[25] Ibid, 26-27.

[26] Ibid, 32.

[27] Ibid, 14.

maintained pure bloodlines. This ensured a high rate of nobility among the villages and little

distinction between nobles and commoners. This also meant that the majority of people in the

region owned the land they farmed. This sense of ownership led to increased productivity.

Conversely, in the lowland regions of Spain, there were far fewer nobles, resulting in a less

equitable distribution of wealth and land ownership and higher social stratification.

Regional agricultural practices also contributed to low social stratification in the Navarre.

Peasants employed an ancient, small spade called a *laya*, instead of a plow as the *laya* was better

suited for the steep terrain and small plots. The small size of the *laya* meant that all citizens,

including women, had to contribute to the planting and maintenance of the fields. This

established women as an integral part of society in the Navarre. Since women were accustomed

to taking part in all aspects of society, when the men were away fighting, there was little

disruption of agricultural production.[28]

The economy of the Navarre ensured insurgent access to resources. The *fuero* allowed

the Navarre to establish its own fiscal policy. The region established its own customs system

which provided significant revenue. The Navarrese exported a tremendous amount of raw

materials, such as wool, to France and levied its own tariffs, separate from those of Spain. This

income allowed the region to maintain its economic independence from the rest of Spain and to

fix local prices to protect small farmers and landless laborers.[29] The independent customs policy

also contributed to a healthy smuggling industry which contributed to the widespread availability

----

[28] Ibid, 28-29.
[29] Ibid, 36.

of weapons in the region and a well developed system of clandestine routes and methods suitable for the conduct of the insurgency. There were more guns available in the Navarre than in any other region in Spain. During the French occupation, the region's economic independence provided the insurgency with excellent access to resources.

Economic independence was further facilitated by the physical composition of the villages. The population was widely dispersed among numerous small independent villages comprised of large *caserios*. The *caserio* was a large stone house designed to "contain the family, the animals, the tools, and the harvest."[30] Inhabitants possessed all of the necessities for survival within the *caserios*. So, in addition to being somewhat naturally fortified positions, the villages relied less upon trade with regions outside the mountains.

For the French, the geographic and social factors proved too difficult an obstacle to overcome. The low social stratification provided horizontal solidarity which prevented the French from using the distribution of wealth and privilege to combat resistance as they did in the urban areas.[31] Social and economic inequalities were the foundations of the French Revolution. In the Navarre, the low social stratification and economic independence offered no social, economic, or political seams for the French to exploit—the French Revolution had little appeal. To make matters worse, the French attempted to dissolve the system of regional independence granted by the *fuero*. This act constituted a direct attack against the fiercely independent Navarrese.

_____

[30] Ibid, 13.
[31] Ibid, 14-15.

Much like the Chinese Nationalists a century and a half later, the French were never able to establish a secure foothold in the mountains and were forced to concede the region to the guerillas. From their prosperous and protected refuge, the Spanish guerrillas continued to tie up French forces that may have otherwise been used during the invasion of Russia, as well as threaten French lines of communication between France and forces fighting the British in Portugal. In 1813, Napoleon suffered defeats in both Russia and Portugal. Due to the deleterious effects of the guerilla campaign in Spain, Napoleon's Peninsula Campaign became widely known as his "Spanish Ulcer."[32]

The political, cultural, and economic self reliance of the society and ruggedness of the physical geography all combined to provide an ideal physical and social sanctuary for the Spanish guerillas. Despite living a largely agrarian existence, the Spanish were able to develop a complex system of physical and social sanctuary. Modern insurgents have access to considerable advances in technology, information sharing, and social structures to create considerably more complex sanctuaries.

Virtual Sanctuary

Information has always been a crucial component in warfare. Ho Chi Minh and Vo Nguyen Giap effectively used information to leverage the media and international opinion as a

---

[32] BBC.co.uk, *Napoleon Bonaparte, from Empire to Waterloo*, (created October 7, 2004), http://www.bbc.co.uk/dna/h2g2/A2875421, accessed April 16, 2008.

form of sanctuary during their struggle to obtain Vietnamese independence. Modern information technology and practices made available by the information revolution, however, have expanded the means and potency of information as a weapon.

For the insurgent, the anonymity and security provided by modern communication and information technologies serves as a form of virtual sanctuary from which insurgents gain critical resources and protection from counterinsurgent action. Both of these dynamics can, and have been, applied by insurgencies to both increase their security and resilience to counterinsurgent actions, enhance the effectiveness and efficiency of clandestine guerilla tactics, and communicate with a wider, global audience.

As communication technology advances in the form of digital media devices, cellular phones, and internet connectivity, both access to information and the speed with which information can be transmitted is increasing exponentially. In their Rand publication: *The Future of Terror, Crime and Militancy*, John Arquilla and David Ronfeldt suggest that the information revolution has had two significant impacts on the nature of conflict, the strengthening of network forms of organization over hierarchical structures and the increasing dependence on information and communications.[33] The increased access to and speed of information allows insurgencies to abandon traditional hierarchical organizations for a more dispersed, decentralized, and amorphous structure conjoined by a virtual network of modern information technologies. This networked organizational structure and more efficient sharing of information also greatly enhances the

---

[33] John Arquilla and David Ronfeldt, *Networks and Netwars: the Future of Terror, Crime*, and Militancy, (Santa Monica: RAND, 2001), 1.

security and command of insurgencies which, traditionally, have relied upon cellular organizational structures and clandestine guerilla communications as a means of security. Instead of relying upon physical means of communications such as messengers, dead drops, or meetings—all vulnerable to counterinsurgent disruption—modern insurgent leaders can now send instructions via email, electronic dead-drops at an internet café, disposable cell phones, encoded innocuously on a website, or transmitted though a video-taped message provided to the media.[34] Insurgents may not know specifically from whom they receive direction and, thus, if captured, cannot reveal the identities of their superiors.

The increased speed of information and power to network provided by modern information technology also exponentially increases an insurgency's access to resources. Within the virtual sanctuary provided by modern technology, insurgencies can leverage multiple sources of modern media to reach diverse audiences worldwide. This allows insurgents to access funds electronically, coordinate recruiting efforts outside the boundaries of their physical sanctuary, gather information on their adversaries, and to mobilize a group or Diaspora to action.[35]

The Zapatista movement in Mexico during the 1990s is an example of the use of virtual sanctuary. On 1 January 1994, an army of indigenous people initiated an uprising in the southern Mexican state of Chiapas. The Zapatista National Liberation Army (EZLN) seized the city of

---

[34] Thomas, *Cyber Silhouettes*, 32-45.
[35] Ibid, 37-44.

San Cristobal de las Casas and several other small towns.[36] The Mexican government responded with a conventional air and ground military offensive.

Taking a page from Ernesto "Che" Guevara's *"foco"*[37] theory of guerilla warfare, the Zapatistas hoped that the example of armed struggle would motivate the peasants and disadvantaged throughout Mexico, sparking a revolution that would at best, overthrow the government and, at worst, force the government to abandon economic policies that disadvantaged the poor. With this armed struggle in mind, the Zapatistas formed into dispersed battalion-sized formations under centralized command and control and attempted to stand their ground against the Mexican army forces.[38] The dispersed forces and centralized command and control proved disastrous as the Zapatistas were not able to effectively mass against the Mexican Army forces and, consequently, suffered numerous casualties and were forced to abandon the cities they captured.[39] The EZLN fled to the physical sanctuary of the jungles and mountains

With the failure of their armed efforts, the EZLN moved their struggle into the information realm. When the Zapatistas initiated their revolution, they posted a printed declaration of war against the Mexican government calling for the liberation of the people of

---

[36] Arquilla and Ronfeldt, *The Zapatista Social Netwar in Mexico*, p. 1.

[37] Ernesto "Che" Guevara, *Che Guevara on Guerrilla Warfare*, ed. Harries-Clichy Peterson, (New York: Frederick A. Praeger Publisher, 1961). While both Mao and Che understood the role of popular support during an insurgency, they differed on how to best achieve popular support. Mao believed in mobilizing the masses prior to waging open warfare against government forces. Che, on the other hand, believed that a well armed and trained core group of guerrillas could "spark" the masses to action by attaining military victories against government forces.

[38] Arquilla et al., *The Zapatista Social Netwa in Mexicor*, 46-47.

[39] Ibid.

Chiapas. This declaration was quickly transmitted through a student's call to CNN and from there, to the world.[40] As media outlets flooded to Chiapas to report on the situation, the EZLN took full advantage to publish communiqués, letters, and newspapers detailing alleged human rights abuses committed by the Mexican forces. The information was propagated via television, radio, print, and the internet. The EZLN also utilized an eloquent spokesperson known as "Subcomandante Marcos" to declare their grievances and anti-globalization positions.

The EZLN's media offensive was extremely effective in limiting the Mexican government's response and garnering international support for the insurgent movement. Human rights activists, indigenous rights activists, fellow anti-globalizationist organizations, and numerous nongovernmental organizations (NGOs) mobilized to voice their support for the EZLN. The network of NGOs and other supporters used fax-writing campaigns, public assemblies, press conferences, interviews, and other measures to pressure the Mexican government for a cease-fire, the withdrawal of the Mexican army, and access to monitor conditions in the conflict zone.[41] As a result, on January 12, the Mexican president agreed to enter negotiations and halted combat operations. The network of organizations and the virtual space through which the insurgents communicated, organized, and mobilized successfully provided the EZLN with refuge from the Mexican government as well as virtual access to international resources and support.

---

[40] Harry Cleaver, "The Zapatistas and the Electronic Fabric of Struggle," *Zapatista: Reinventing Revolution in Mexico*, ed. John Holloway and Eloina Pelaez, (London: Pluto Press, 1998), 82

[41] Arquilla et al, *The Zapatista Social Netwar in Mexico*, 50-51.

Computer, cell-phone, and other information technologies have advanced considerably since the Zapatista revolt. Today's insurgent can potentially access the internet and other communication networks from nearly anywhere. These capabilities provide modern insurgents with an unprecedented level of refuge from counterinsurgent action and access to resources. No longer constrained by physical contact, insurgents leverage the anonymity and security of the internet to recruit, plan, train, and fund their operations. Though not invincible, these virtual methods are much more challenging to identify, interdict, and exploit.

Legal Sanctuary

A fourth form of sanctuary is provided by both external laws governing the world order and internal laws within sovereign states. Legal sanctuary is the refuge and access to resources provided by laws limiting exercise of power. These laws are intended to protect the rights of law abiding citizens, but are exploited by insurgents and criminal elements. The primary utility of legal sanctuary is intensifying the protection from counterinsurgent influence and providing secure access to critical resources within an insurgent system of sanctuary. There is a long history of insurgencies using international borders as protection from counterinsurgent influence, but that is not the only form of legal sanctuary. Insurgents may also take refuge in legal protections within states, limitations imposed by national codes of justice, constitutional laws, and international laws and statutes.

Though a comprehensive discussion of international geopolitics, law, and world order is beyond the scope of this paper, the concept of legal sanctuary requires the establishment of some foundational concepts. This paper generally accepts the modernist theory that sovereign states with internationally recognized boundaries remain the dominant unit of action in international politics, but also acknowledges the validity of many post-modernist concepts which suggest that globalization is changing the nature of traditional, state-centric power relations.[42] As the predominant unit of political action, states generally act in accordance with accepted rules of conduct or action prescribed or generally accepted as binding.[43] These international rules of conduct generally deal with ensuring stability and order by restraining or limiting a state's exercise of power.[44] The Peace of Westphalia, which refers to the pair of treaties ending the Thirty Years War in 1648, is most well known for establishing the current international system of sovereign states, legal equality between states, and non-intervention of one state in the internal affairs of another.[45]

The existence of sovereign state borders has provided insurgencies with the most common form of legal sanctuary. Insurgents often take advantage of the counterinsurgent's

---

[42] Gearoid O Tuathail, "De-Territorialised Threats and Global Dangers: Geopolitics and Risk Society," *Boundaries, Territory, and Postmodernity*, ed. David Newman, (Portland, OR: F. Cass, 1999), 17-19.

[43] From the Merriam Webster Dictionary definition of "law," http://www.merriam-webster.com/dictionary/law, accessed April 16, 2008.

[44] Tuathail, "De-Territorialised Threats and Global Dangers," 17.

[45] The text of the 1648 Treaty of Westphalia can be accessed at: http://www.yale.edu/lawweb/avalon/westphal.htm, (accessed April 16, 2008)

inability to violate the border of a neighboring sovereign country. In his study of transnational

sanctuary, Thomas Bruscino cites several examples:

> "In the Greek Civil War (1946-1949), the communist rebels enjoyed the use of
> sanctuaries in Albania, Yugoslavia, and Bulgaria. The communist insurgents
> fighting the British-supported government in Malaya from 1948 to 1960 had
> some sanctuaries in neighboring Thailand. Anti-French rebels in Indochina
> (1946-1954) could look to China for supply and refuge, and anti-French fighters
> in the Algerian War of Independence (1954-1962) had sanctuaries in Morocco
> and Tunisia."[46]

In the modern American experience, the North Vietnamese used transnational sanctuary

within Laos and Cambodia to both move troops and supplies from North to South Vietnam and to

rest and refit their forces.[47] Additionally, as mentioned earlier, the Taliban have used

transnational sanctuary within the sovereign borders of Pakistan to rearm, retrain, and as a base

for launching offensives into Afghanistan. It is widely believed that insurgents are also

leveraging sanctuary within Syria and Iran to fight American and Iraqi forces in Iraq.[48]

Legal sanctuary is not isolated to manipulating the international state system to provide

legal cover for physical sanctuary. Insurgents can manipulate the laws within a state as legal

sanctuary, as well. This is particularly effective in Western-style democracies which protect the

rights of citizens by placing constitutional limits on the national government's use of power.

Under this protective legal umbrella, insurgents are free to recruit, secure funding, train, and

---

[46] Thomas A. Bruscino, *Out of Bounds: Transnational Sanctuary in Irregular Warfare*, (Fort Leavenworth: Combat Studies Institute, 2006), 7.

[47] Ibid, 9.

[48] Angel Rabasa et al., *The Global Jihadist Movement*, (Santa Monica: RAND, 2006), 138-145.

operate. David Galula cited this as a common tactic in the early stages of an insurgency. He claimed that an incipient insurgency will wage what he terms "cold revolutionary war" by operating legally and non-violently within a sovereign state. The government is unable to prove that the potential risks posed by the budding insurgency warrant the efforts and sacrifices required to defeat the insurgency. Galula suggested that the insurgent intentionally slows the transition from peace to war in order to leverage this advantage over the counterinsurgent.[49]

The current debate in the United States surrounding the USA PATRIOT Act exemplifies the difficulty in combating legal sanctuary. Signed into law shortly after the September 11th attacks, the PATRIOT Act expanded the authorities of US law enforcement agencies to search telephone, email, medical, and financial records, and it also eased the restrictions on foreign intelligence gathering within the United States for the purpose of fighting terrorism.[50] President George W. Bush also issued a secret presidential order authorizing the National Security Agency (NSA) to eavesdrop on international phone calls and email communications that originate from or are received within the United States without the normally-required court approval.[51] Passage of the PATRIOT Act and discovery of the warrantless surveillance ignited considerable resistance

---

[49] Galula, *Counterinsurgency Warfare*, 63-64.

[50] 107th Congress, 1st Session, *Uniting and Strengthening America by Providing Appropriate Tools Required to Intercept and Obstruct Terrorism (USA PATRIOT ACT) Act of 2001*, (Electronic Privacy Information Center, October 24, 2001) http://epic.org/privacy/terrorism/hr3162.html, (accessed April 16, 2008)

[51] Media Matters, "Candidates still not asked about wiretaps, FISA, or telecom immunity in debates," (January 24, 2008), http://mediamatters.org/items/200801240006, (accessed March 9, 2008).

from many citizens and civil-rights organizations who feared the act enabled abuses of power that may infringe upon constitutionally guaranteed individual liberties.[52]

The warrantless surveillance program, in particular, sparked considerable debate and litigation against the government and against private sector communications companies who assisted in collecting or recording emails and telephone calls. Members of the US Congress initiated legislation requiring more significant Congressional and judicial oversight of the program and, in 2006 a federal judge in Detroit declared the warrantless wire-tapping program unconstitutional.[53] At the time of this writing, the issue remains unresolved.

As the debate over the USA PATRIOT Act and domestic surveillance plan continues, reports suggest that foreign terrorist organizations like Al Qaeda and Hamas have established cells within the Unites States.[54] These cells use the legal sanctuary of US civil liberties to collect information, recruit, solicit funds, and conduct operations.

Another form of legal sanctuary is that caused by international "peer pressure" upon the counterinsurgent state. During the Zapatista revolt in Mexico, international consternation about alleged human rights abuses played a significant role in the cancelation of the Mexican Army's

---

[52] Larry Abramson and Maria Godoy, "The Patriot Act: Key Controversies," National Public Radio website (December 16, 2005), http://www.npr.org/news/specials/patriotact/patriotactdeal.html, (accessed March 10, 2008)

[53] Larry Abramson, "Bush's Wiretaps Ruled Unconstitutional," National Public Radio website (August 17, 2006), http://www.npr.org/templates/story/story.php?storyId=5665192, (accessed March 9, 2008)

[54] The Associated Press, "Military Commander Sees Increased Al Qaeda Threat in US," The International Herald Tribune (July 24, 2007), http://www.iht.com/articles/ap/2007/07/24/america/NA-GEN-US-Terror-Threat.php, (accessed April 16, 2008).

offensive. As a responsible member of the international community, Mexico was obligated to provide transparency and access to Chiapas for the NGOs, human rights organizations and other members of the international community. Failure to do so would have reflected poorly upon the Mexican government and aroused further international suspicion of wrongdoing. The Zapatistas took advantage of the forced lull in government COIN actions to reorganize and adapt. The legal sanctuary provided by international pressure on the counterinsurgent Mexican government, combined with the virtual sanctuary offered by modern information technology, ensured the survival of the insurgency.

The synergy created by insurgents combining the various forms of sanctuary—physical, social, virtual, and legal--presents a highly complex and adaptive system which limits the ability of counterinsurgent forces to effectively deny refuge and resources to insurgents. The next chapter will describe what constitutes a system and what makes it complex and adaptive.

Chapter 3: Sanctuary as a Component of a Complex Adaptive System

Systems theory is being integrated into current joint doctrine. It advocates a systems approach to planning to help planners identify elements of operational design.[55] JP 3-0, *Joint Operations*, defines a system as "a functionally related group of elements forming a complex

---

[55] Joint Publication 5-0, *Joint Operation Planning*, (December 26, 2006), III-17.

whole."[56] It suggests that a system consists of nodes[57] and links[58]-- the variables and linkages of a complex adaptive system -- which may be targeted to achieve effects. The concept of targeting elements of the system suggests that one must first understand the nodes and links—their structure, purpose, actions, motivations, and relationships between one another—in order to have an informed idea as to what effects actions on them may have. Nodes are further sub-categorized into interrelated groups, specifically, Political, Military, Economic, Social, Information, and Infrastructure (PMESII).

The concept of sanctuary, with its different facets and multiple dimensions, is best viewed as a complex system of nodes and relationships between the nodes. The geographic, social, technological, economic, legal, and military components are all nodes within the system whose roles and behaviors are shaped by the relationships between them. The multitude of nodes and links also give the system of sanctuary a high degree of complexity and potential for adaptation. This chapter will explain complex and adaptive systems and apply a systems analysis to the Spanish system of sanctuary during Napoleon's Peninsula Campaign and the Zapatista Revolution in Mexico to demonstrate the complex and adaptive nature of sanctuary.

---

[56] Joint Publication 3-0, *Joint Operations,* (September 17, 2006), II-21.

[57] System Nodes are tangible elements within a system that can be "targeted" for action. (JP 3-0, IV-4).

[58] Links are the behavioral or functional relationships between nodes (JP 3-0, p. IV-4).

Complexity

Complexity has many definitions, most of which indicate two components: several variables and significant interdependence among them.[59] TRADOC Pam 525-FW-X, *Commanders Appreciation and Campaign Design*, categorizes these as Structural Complexity and Interactive Complexity. A system with many parts has great structural complexity. The greater the number of linkages between the parts, and the freedom of action of each part increases the system's interactive complexity. A system may be structurally complex, but not interactively so and vice versa. For example, many modern machines such as automobiles possess many parts, but the behaviors and relationships between each part are predictable. These systems are complicated, but not necessarily complex. The terms "parts" and "linkages" are synonymous with the terms "nodes" and "links" from joint doctrine.

In the case of insurgent sanctuary, the physical and social sanctuary in Napoleonic Spain contained significant structural and interactive complexity. Figure 1 is a simple systems model of the Navarre Region that shows various critical nodes within political, social, economic, military, and physical infrastructure subsystems and the links between them. The diagram is not a final product but, rather, a starting point to facilitate understanding of the system. Changes in behavior among the various nodes will require changes in the system model. Additionally, further analysis

---

[59] In *Harnessing Complexity*, (New York: Basic Books, 2000), Robert Axelrod and Michael Cohen define complexity as indicat[ing] that the system consists of parts which interact in ways that heavily influence the probabilities of later events. In *The Logic of Failure*, (New York: Metropolitan Books, 1996), Dietrich Dorner defines it as "the existence of many interdependent variables in a given system. The more variables and the greater their interdependence, the greater the complexity."

would reveal more complex links between the various nodes in each subsystem or additional

nodes within each subsystem.

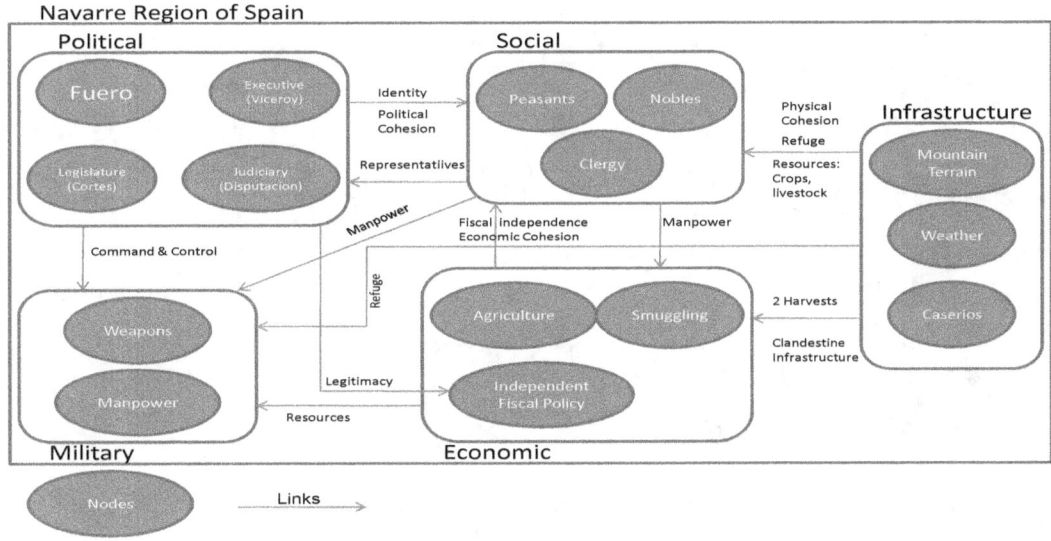

Figure 1: Internal system analysis of Navarre region during Napoleon's 1808 Spanish Campaign

Furthermore, the internal system in Navarre was merely a node within a larger system.

Many of the nodes and links in the Navarre's internal and external systems contributed to the

insurgents sanctuary. As shown in figure 2, the quantity of nodes displays significant structural

complexity while the interaction between the nodes displays interactive complexity. The

system's interactive complexity was largely a function of the human nodes in the system. The

geographic and environmental nodes do not have a high degree of "freedom of action," as

weather patterns and geography are relatively fixed, but the human social factors do. Under

Spanish rule, the people of the Navarre provided limited support to the king in exchange for

relative autonomy under the *fuero* constitution. The populace did this out of choice and was free

to change its behavior at any time. By contrast, the terrain was not free to change its behavior.

Though the terrain contributed to high structural complexity, it did not contribute to the systems

interactive complexity.

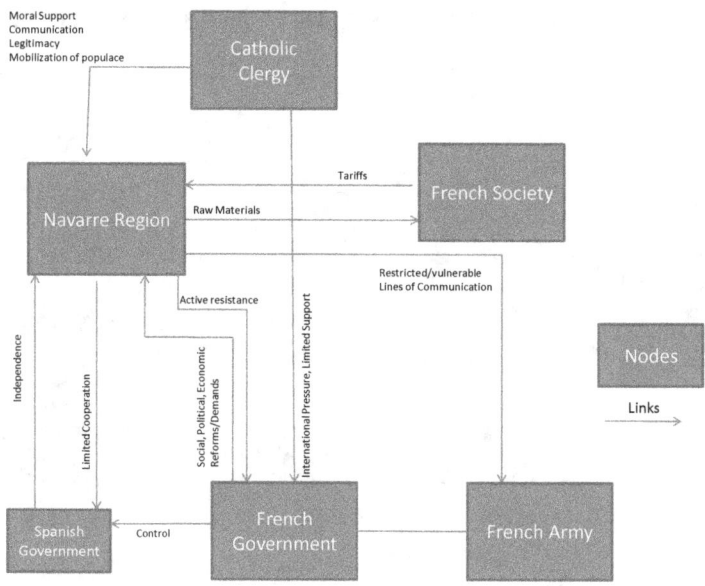

Figure 2: External system analysis of Navarre region during Napoleon's 1808 Spanish campaign.

Understanding the nodes and links is crucial to operating within a complex environment. Increased understanding of the insurgents system of sanctuary allows operational planners to predict behavior within the system and determine what effects their intervention within the system may cause.[60] The behavior and traditions of the populace in Spain's lowlands differed remarkably from those in the mountains.

Figure 3 demonstrates how in the lowlands high social stratification laid the seeds of discontent between peasants and nobles. The nobles "feared the [peasant] mob more than the

---

[60] Axelrod & Cohen, *Harnessing Complexity*, 14-15.

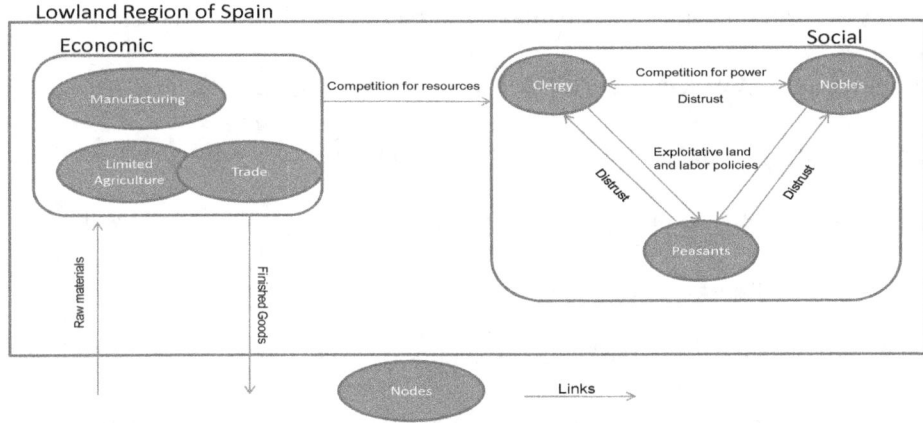

Figure 3: System analysis of the lowland regions in Spain during Napoleon's 1808 Spanish campaign.

French and were easily induced to cooperate."[61] Additionally, the economy in the lowlands was

not independent and self-sufficient. Society relied heavily on importing raw materials and

exporting finished goods. This allowed the French to exploit these seams to pit the nobles,

peasants, and clergy against one another. In the lowlands, the French revolutionary ideology of

social and financial equality had significant appeal to the populace.

The French incorrectly applied their understanding of the social system in the Spanish

lowlands to their interventions in the Navarre. Much to their chagrin, the French soon discovered

that the actions they took in the lowlands to eliminate resistance resulted in a much different

reaction in the highlands. This was largely due to the freedom of action of the human nodes

within the system. This freedom of action greatly enhanced the complexity of the problem for the

French.

---

[61] Tone, *The Fatal Knot*, 16.

Modern systems of insurgent sanctuary display even more complexity. Access to virtual sanctuary and the increased impact of legal sanctuary due to globalization greatly increases the level of structural and interactive complexity. In Mexico, the Zapatistas not only possessed the physical sanctuary of the jungle and the mountains, but the virtual sanctuary of the news media and internet and the legal sanctuary of the international community.

As figure 4 below illustrates, sanctuary for the EZLN was largely a function of the physical sanctuary provided to the EZLN by the towns, mountains and jungles of Chiapas. During the initial military offensive, the Mexican Army successfully recaptured the towns and placed pressure on the EZLN forces in the jungles and mountains. By leveraging the global reach of modern information technology, the Zapatistas were able establish an effective virtual sanctuary to compensate for their diminishing physical sanctuary. Modern information technology also provided a conduit to NGOs and other members of the international community who, in turn, provided legal sanctuary and resources to the EZLN. As a result, the complexity of the situation facing the government of Mexico compounded exponentially. The new nodes added to the system by the EZLN provided a form of legal refuge from Mexican governmental action.

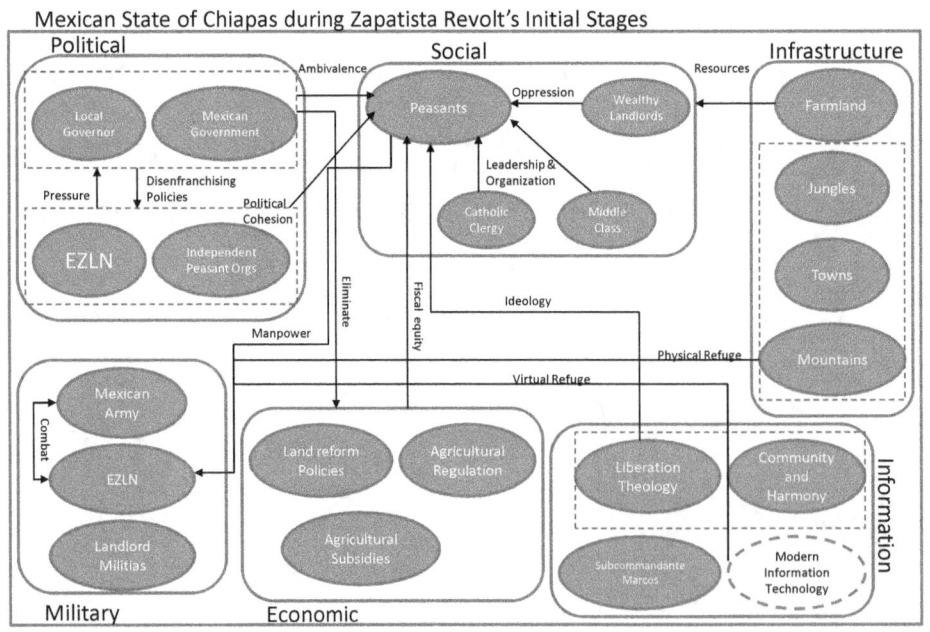

Figure 4: Internal system analysis of the Mexican State of Chiapas during the Zapatista Revolt

With the additional global scrutiny, the Mexican government found its response options

constrained. The Mexican government could no longer focus only on a military response against

an isolated hierarchical opponent, but rather had to adapt and apply all elements of national power

to face a widespread, networked collection of actors.

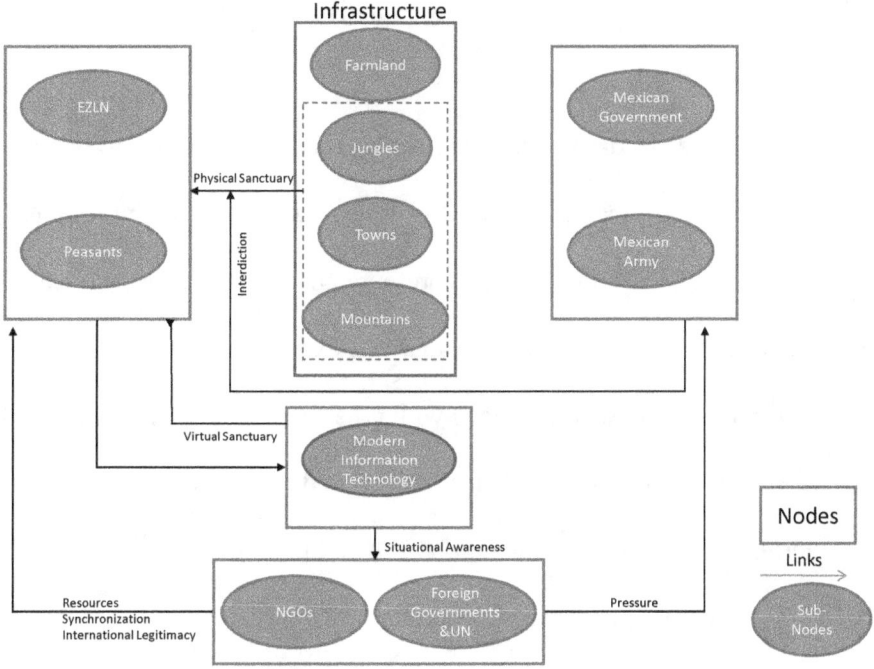

Figure 5: External system analysis of the Mexican state of Chiapas during the Zapatista revolt

The transformation of the EZLN's system of sanctuary highlights the second component

of complex adaptive systems—adaptation.

Adaptation

In addition to complexity, complex adaptive systems also "exhibit coherence under change, via conditional action and anticipation, and they do so without central direction."[62] This ability to adapt to change creates a dilemma for planners as it makes the behavior of elements within the system nonlinear and difficult to predict.[63] Elements within the system may exhibit different behavior than previously observed. They may establish new interactions with other variables. New variables may form.

In Chiapas, after the initial 10 days of failed military combat operations, the Zapatistas shifted the conflict to the information realm. Rather than inspiring the poor within Mexico, they inspired international sympathizers with the power to pressure and influence the Mexican government. True to the concept of adaptation, the Zapatistas exhibited different behavior than previously observed and established new interactions with other variables. The newly established virtual sanctuary provided by modern information technology and the legal sanctuary provided by the cooperation of numerous international organizations allowed them to adapt and expand their system to nodes they would not otherwise have access to.

---

[62] John H. Holland, *Hidden Order: How Adaptation Builds Complexity*, (Reading: Addison-Wesley Publishing Co., 1995), 55.

[63] Axelrod & Cohen, *Harnessing Complexity*, 14.

Impact of Complexity and Adaptation to Operational Design

Complexity and adaptation are the bane of operational planners. By definition, complexity and adaptation add disorder to the system planners are attempting to impose some semblance of order and control upon. Continuous change within the system being studied forces planners to continually reassess and reframe their understanding of the system. Previous assumptions and courses of action will likely have to change. The speed with which these adaptations occur adds to the complexity. The planners' processes must maintain the flexibility and responsiveness to observe and react to changes within the system before the system changes yet again. As stated in the TRADOC PAM 525-FW-X, "the study of interactively complex systems must be systemic rather than systematic, holistic rather than reductionist, and qualitative rather than quantitative, and must use different heuristic approaches rather than the scientific method."[64]

Chapter 4: Commanders Appreciation and Campaign Design

Current US joint doctrine offers an introductory explanation of systems theory. A debate exists among military leaders how to apply systems theory to operational planning. Commander's Appreciation and Campaign Design (CACD) is an emerging concept in response to the complexity of modern warfare. TRADOC Pam 525-FW-X defines CACD as a "method to gain a systemic appreciation, or understanding, of a complex adaptive problem and design a

---

[64] TRADOC Pam 525-FW-X, *Commander's Appreciation and Campaign Design* (2007), 5.

broad approach for its resolution."[65] CACD offers a method to operationalize systems theory in joint doctrine by providing a holistic, systemic and qualitative cognitive process. Instead of dictating "what to think" the CACD approach suggests "how to think." Applied properly, CACD allows planners to analyze and identify the problem while consciously making an effort to reduce bias and while analyzing the system. Additionally, CACD leads planners to consider and account for multiple threats, both conventional and asymmetric. Finally, CACD advocates a cyclical, continuous approach of analysis, learning, reframing, and adaptation necessary for complex adaptive environments. This chapter will illustrate the utility of applying CACD to complex and adaptive problems such as insurgent sanctuary.

Systemic Operational Design (SOD) is the foundation of CACD. Retired Israeli general Shimon Naveh is one of the progenitors of SOD. In his 1997 book *In Pursuit of Military Excellence: The Evolution of Operational Theory*, Gen Naveh champions systemic processes applied at the operational level of war as the bridge between tactics and strategy. He claims that the search for a decisive 'Battle of Destruction' (*Vernichtungsschlach*) has biased military theory for centuries towards tactical innovation at the expense of operational art.[66] Gen Naveh cites the Soviet deep operation theory (*Glubokaia Operatsiia*) as a return to systemic operational theory.

Since publishing *In Pursuit of Military Excellence*, Gen Naveh has continued to develop his theory of SOD and codified it into two general processes: System Framing and Operational

---

[65] Ibid, 3-4.

[66] Shimon Naveh, *In Pursuit of Military Excellence: The Evolution of Operational Theory*, (Portland: Frank Cass Publishers), 16.

Framing[67]. In general, the first process is the unbiased analysis of the system and the second is the analysis and establishment of the mission within that system.

A problem with the current theory of SOD is that it is largely conceptual and lacks sufficient systematic processes to translate it into action for planners. Commander's Appreciation and Campaign Design offers commanders a cognitive model to operationalize the SOD concepts and nest them with current planning doctrine.

The title itself provides the link to SOD theory. *Commander's Appreciation* is used to "describe the commander's understanding of the situation."[68] *Campaign Design* "produces a framed problem (understanding) and a framework for problem solving, and it identifies the required capabilities and resources"[69]

System Framing: Commander's Appreciation

The process of System Framing seeks to gain a holistic understanding of the system. System Framing is similar to the Joint Intelligence Preparation of the Operational Environment (JIPOE) process of defining the battlespace environment except it is more inductive and inclusive. Planners use guidance from higher level headquarters to establish the initial boundaries of the system being analyzed. Through discourse that eschews process in favor of analysis and

---

[67] LTC William T. Sorrells et al., *Systemic Operational Design: An Introduction*, (Fort Leavenworth: United States Army Command and General Staff College School of Advanced Military Studies, 2005), 23.

[68] TRADOC Pam 525-FW-X, 13.

[69] Ibid.

learning, planners outline their understanding of the system by identifying nodes and linkages between the nodes. Through this analysis, they may modify their initial boundaries and reframe the system.

The system is analyzed without regard to the friendly mission or goals in order to understand the dynamics inherent within the system, free of bias. This difference is subtle, but crucial. Instead of analyzing the system with preconceived notions of how to think about the problem (i.e. mission and commander's intent), planners approach the analysis with the attitude of "what have we learned and how should we think about it?"[70] This bottom-up approach is the essence of problem setting and analysis in CACD.

A key sub-step of system framing is "Rival as Rationale."[71] This involves identifying the rival in the system—the fundamental problem either causing instability within the system or with the potential to destabilize it.[72] This process differs from the JIPOE step of evaluating the threat in that it takes a holistic approach towards analyzing the threat and does not focus on identifying a single, state-centric threat with established doctrine. Where JIPOE attempts to reduce the threat to predictable doctrine and limited courses of action, SOD/CACD attempts to understand various threats and their relationships within the system. Also, in SOD/CACD, the threat evaluation is an integral part of the System Framing. Current joint doctrine separates the analysis of the threat from that of the environment. This is a weakness in the current method in that planners may fail

---

[70] BG (RET) Huba Wass de Czege & LTC Reb Yancey. *Why Systemic Operational Design: Unified Quest/Irregular Warfare Study* slides, April 2006, slide 11.

[71] LTC William T. Sorrells et al., *Systemic Operational Design: An Introduction*, 23.,

to identify or account for key linkages between the threat and other nodes in the environment as they establish their doctrinal template. The end result of System Framing is an initial system framework, an unbiased and neutral understanding of the various nodes, linkages, and threats within the system, and an understanding of the various potentials within the system. Unfortunately, operational planners will rarely have all of the information required to form a complete understanding of the system. Establishing an initial node and link diagram, however, allows planners to identify knowledge gaps and take measures to fill in the missing pieces. This may often require intelligence, political, financial, or diplomatic assets outside of the planners normal purview. Appreciating this fact early in the process gives planners time to coordinate for resources.

When analyzing an insurgency's system of sanctuary, framing the system involves establishing a comprehensive node and link analysis. Analyzing the rival in the system involves analyzing which nodes and links provide protection from counterinsurgent action and access to resources.[73] This more inclusive type of reasoning is especially important when dealing with the complexity posed by insurgents leveraging multiple forms of sanctuary These open-ended questions force planners to consider the system from several different angles. Based upon this

---

[72] Ibid, slide 12.

[73] Robert D. Lamb, *Ungoverned Areas and Threats from Safe Havens*, (Office of the Deputy Assistant Secretary of Defense for Policy Planning, OUSD(P), 2007), 2. This report published by the Office of the Undersecretary of Defense for Policy (OUSD(P)) offers an excellent analytical framework for problem analysis in dealing with sanctuary.[73] The report asks the question "What makes safe havens possible?" and lists four focus areas: 1) Geographical considerations: What areas could be used for safe havens? 2) Political considerations: How is the area governed, 3) Civil considerations: How hospitable is

analysis, planners may form a more complete understanding of the problem than if they began with an initial assumption based simply upon geographic or political boundaries.

The system node and link analyses of the Zapatista Revolt (figures 4 and 5) illustrate the process of System Framing. Analyzing the system models identifies not only the physical sanctuary provided by the terrain, but the financial, social, and political independence that established the social sanctuary. (figures 6 and 7).

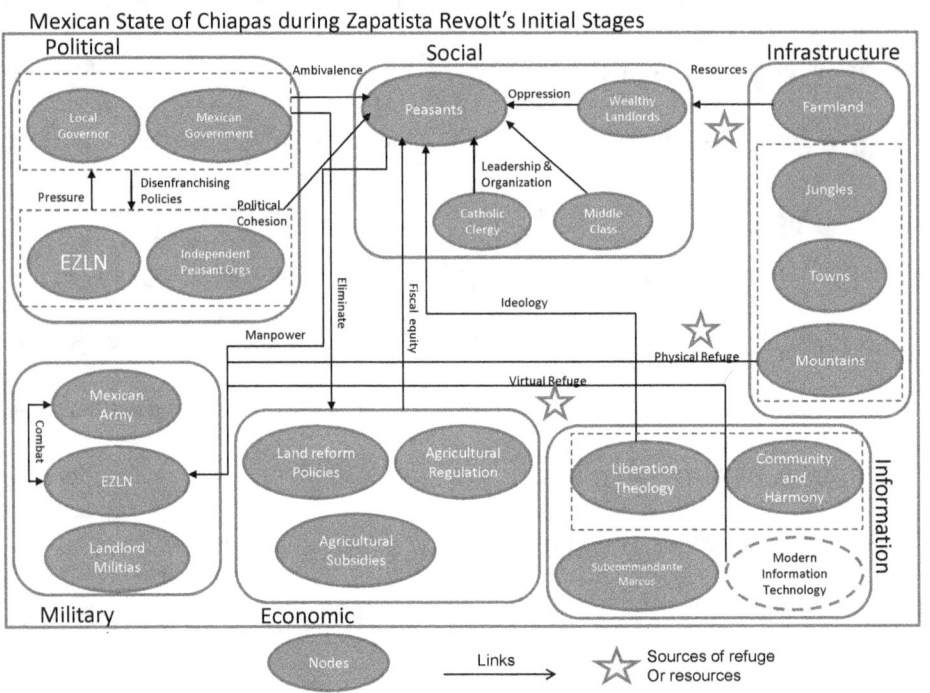

Figure 6: Sanctuary analysis of the Zapatista Revolt internal to Chiapas

the local population? And 4) Resource considerations: What is available to facilitate illicit operations? http://www.cissm.umd.edu/papers/files/ugash_report_final.pdf, (accessed 16 April, 2008).

Adaptation of Sanctuary in Chiapas

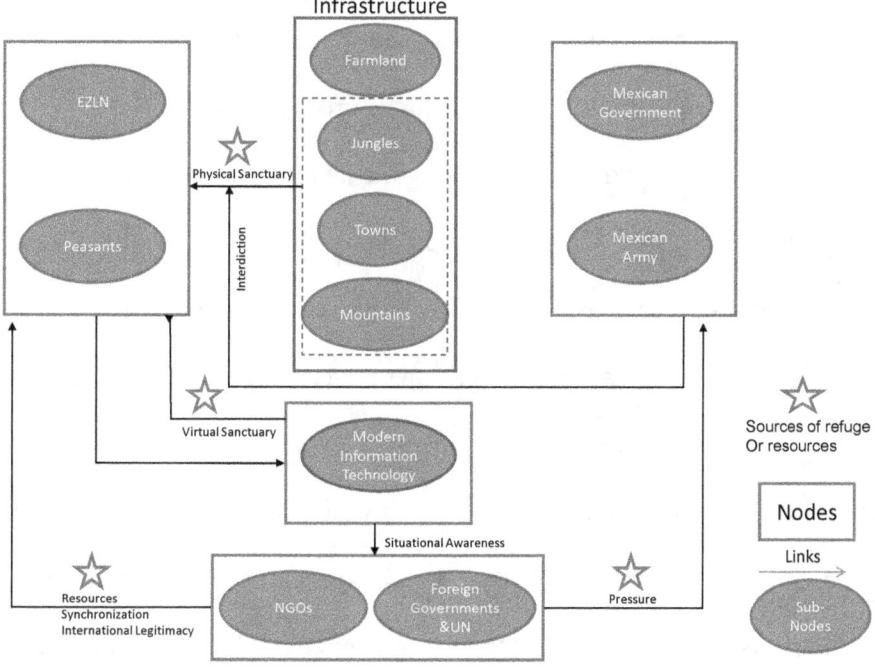

Figure 7: Sanctuary analysis of the Chiapas Revolt external to Chiapas

Applying SOD/CACD is about gaining an understanding of the system. Asking the questions "why" and "how" these nodes and relationships provide refuge and access to resources leads to additional insights and understanding of the system. Specifically, analysis of the system provides insight into the root causes of the insurgent ideology. Chiapas is one of Mexico's poorest states. Since the economy of Chiapas is largely agrarian, farmland is a precious resource in Chiapas as. A feudal system exists in which wealthy landowners with private armies exploit the peasants—fueling a source of tension and instability within Chiapas. To appease the peasants, the Mexican government established laws providing land reform and redistribution and agricultural subsidies. Unfortunately, the Mexican government revoked the land reform policies and subsidies, creating an agricultural and economic crisis in Chiapas.[74]

Understanding why and how eliminating the land reform policies and agricultural subsidies impacted the peasants leads to an appreciation of how the resulting agricultural and economic crisis fueled an ideology of social liberation among the peasants in Chiapas and motivated them to revolt. The addition of information technology to the system allowed the peasants in Chiapas to communicate their ideology to sympathetic international actors who, subsequently, intervened on their behalf, providing virtual and legal sanctuary. The rival in the system was not, in fact, the peasants, but the social, political, and economic inequities that existed in Chiapas. Establishing an operational framework and identifying the rival in the system frames the problem and facilitates the transition from Operational Framing to Campaign Design.

Operational Framing: Campaign Design

Once an initial system frame is established, planners move on to the second major component of SOD/CACD, Operational Framing. This process involves reassessing mission, goals, or national objectives in light of the unbiased understanding of the system and then designing an operational concept to achieve them. During Operational Framing, planners also identify desired operational effects. This concept nests well with current Effects Based

---

[74] Arquilla et al., *The Zapatista Social Netwar in Mexico*, 26-30

Operations concepts in joint doctrine.[75] Based upon planners' understanding of the complex relationships between nodes in the system, planners must account for effects upon multiple nodes within the system and subsequent effects.

Operational Framing is analogous to the application of operational design elements in current joint doctrine;[76] The key difference, however, is the concept of reframing. Based upon the developed understanding of the system, planners may determine that the mission or commander's intent is not feasible and they may need to reframe their goals or objectives. This requires parallel planning between various echelons of headquarters with open and honest discourse. Open and honest discourse is critical because it forces planners to question and, hence, reassess, their understanding of the system and the problem.

This inductive process is the final key element of SOD/CACD and accounts for adaptation within the system. It accepts the fact that planners will find it nearly impossible to obtain a complete understanding of the system, predict every possible behavior within it, or observe and react to every change within it. As such, the concepts of reframing and continual learning are central to SOD/CACD. Current joint doctrine is very linear and final--planners analyze a system in terms of a predetermined problem, apply operational art, and reach a determined end state. SOD/CACD, on the other hand, is a more cyclical approach that attempts to account for second and third order consequences. The initial "end state" is merely a hypothesis

---

[75] See *Commander's Handbook for an Effects Based Approach to Joint Operations*, 24 Feb 2006 for more information on current EBO doctrine.

[76] JP 3-0, *Joint Operations*, IV-6.

based upon the planner's present understanding of the system. This suggests that one must continually reassess the system and the effects of actions upon it. This may lead to reframing the problem and changing the end state hypothesis. This built-in reassessment requires planners to incorporate learning and feedback mechanisms into their operational design.

In dealing with insurgent sanctuary, Operational Framing involves the analysis of how to defeat, mitigate, or contain the refuge and access to resources afforded to the insurgents. Upon establishing a thorough operational framework and understanding which nodes and links provide refuge and access to resources and how they do so, operational planners must identify which nodes or links they can affect. Armed with this understanding of the problem, planners can identify the effects they want to achieve, what resources they have available to apply, and what limitations or constraints may prevent them from doing so. Operational planners must also identify possible second or third order consequences of their actions. Establishment of a thorough operational framework allows them to do. If operational planners know and understand the relationships between various nodes, they can more accurately predict how actions taken upon one will affect the others. Most importantly, properly understanding the system allows planners to reframe their understanding of the problem quicker and more accurately.

In many cases, political, legal, or virtual protections may prevent counterinsurgent operational planners from acting upon one of the nodes. Understanding how these nodes relate to other nodes allows operational planners to either coordinate with other agencies to take action or use other means to monitor and affect the actions of the nodes. For example, prior to OEF, military cooperation with Pakistan was prohibited by sanctions imposed by the Pressler Amendment passed in 1985 in response to Pakistan's nuclear testing. Though the Brownback II Amendment gave the US President the authority to waive the provisions of the Pressler Amendment, it required consultation with various Congressional committees. First understanding the significance of Pakistan's NWFP to Al Qaeda's system of sanctuary and then understanding the impact of the limitations imposed by the Pressler Amendment should have forced operational planners to seek other means to affect Pakistan.

During the Zapatista revolt, the Mexican army was forced to reframe its understanding of the problem. Instead of waging conventional warfare against a group of armed peasants, the Mexican army conducted full-spectrum engagement against a multi-dimensional system of guerrillas, NGOs, the media, and waning popular support. The Army adapted its tactics and devoted its attention to public affairs, psychological operations, improving relations with the NGOs, and correcting human rights issues. The Army decentralized command and control of tactical units and dispersed smaller tactical detachments to blanket the region and deny the enemy physical sanctuary. The army also placed additional emphasis on intelligence gathering, enforced stringent rules of engagement, and developed an information strategy to cultivate better relations with both the media and the local populace.[77] These actions allowed the Mexican army to affect the Zapatista's social, virtual, and legal sanctuaries. Understanding the adaptations in the system allowed the Mexican army to reframe its understanding of the problem and develop a new operational framework to combat the Zapatistas.

Chapter 5: Conclusion

Insurgency is a time-honored form of warfare that allows a weaker opponent to subvert power from a stronger foe. At the turn of the nineteenth century, Spanish guerillas waged an

---

[77] Arquilla et al. *The Zapatista Social Netwar in Mexico*, 74-79.

effective insurgency against the premier army of the period—Napoleon's Grand Armee. In the eighteenth, nineteenth, and twentieth century, numerous European colonies around the globe used insurgent strategies to secure their independence. In each case, sanctuary served as a critical ingredient for the insurgent successes and the importance of all forms of sanctuary was acknowledged by insurgents and counterinsurgents alike.

The significance of insurgent sanctuary is that it allows the insurgent to preserve and protect limited resources and provides protected access to additional resources. Traditionally, insurgencies relied upon the physical and social sanctuaries provided by geography and social conditions. Advances in technology and globalization provide insurgents with additional forms of refuge unavailable during the eighteenth century--virtual and legal. Individually these modern modes of sanctuary consist of a complex array of nodes and links. Collectively, they form a system of great structural and interactive complexity.

The resulting complex, adaptive system forces planners to change the way they analyze and address insurgent sanctuary. Specifically, defeating, mitigating or containing sanctuary requires a holistic, qualitative, and systemic operational approach. SOD/CACD uses systemic framing to gain an appreciation of the entire insurgent system of sanctuary and to understand the behavior of the nodes and links across the entire spectrum of physical, social, virtual, and legal modes. This systemic appreciation facilitates analysis of which nodes and links provide the insurgency with refuge and access to resources. This informed analysis allows operational planners to design a comprehensive campaign to achieve desired effects on these nodes and links.

Defeating, mitigating, or containing sanctuary is particularly salient in the current and future operational environment. Current and future adversaries are able to create and sustain complex and adaptive networks of physical, social, virtual, and legal sanctuary from which they wage global campaigns. As long as insurgents can claim refuge for their ideologies and control the resources necessary to impose their objectives, terrorist organizations will remain a threat to international peace and prosperity. Changing the way we think and act against these complex

adaptive adversaries will enable us to mitigate their impact.

BIBLIOGRAPHY

Arquilla, John and David Ronfeldt, *Networks and Netwars: the Future of Terror, Crime and Militancy*, Santa Monica, CA: National Defense Research Institute and RAND, 2001.

Arquilla, John, David Ronfeldt, Graham E. Fuller, and Melissa Fuller, *The Zapatista Social Netwar in Mexico*, Santa Monica, CA: RAND, 1998.

Axelrod, Robert, and Michael D. Cohen. *Harnessing Complexity.* New York, NY: Basic Books, 2000.

BBC.co.uk, *Napoleon Bonaparte 1805-1821, from Empire to Waterloo*, 2004, http://www.bbc.co.uk/dna/h2g2/A2875421, (accessed April 16, 2008)

Bruscino, Thomas A. *Out of bounds: Transnational Sanctuary in Irregular Warfare.* Fort Leavenworth, KS: Combat Studies Institute Press, 2006.

Dorner, Dietrich. *The Logic of Failure.* New York: Metropolitan Books Henry Holt and Company, 1996.

Dooley, Kevin, *Complex Adaptive Systems: A Nominal Definition*, Arizona State University, online resource, 1996. http://www.eas.asu.edu/~kdooley/casopdef.html

Fall, Bernard B. *Street Without Joy*, Garden City, NY: Schocken Books, 1972.

Galula, David, *Counterinsurgency Warfare: Theory and Practice*, New York, NY: Frederick A. Praeger Publishers, 1964.

Guevarra, Ernesto, *Che Guevara on Guerrilla Warfare*, ed. Harries-Clichy Peterson, New York, NY: Frederick A. Praeger Publisher, 1961.

Hawkins, Scott ed. *Asymmetry and complexity: Selected papers from the 2005 Rowell seminar and the 2005 chief of army's conference.* Canberra, Australia: Land Warfare Studies Centre, 2007.

Ho Chi Minh, *On Revolution: Selected Writings, 1920-66*, ed. Bernard B. Fall, New York, NY: Frederick A. Praeger Publishers, 1967.

Holland, John H. *Hidden Order: How Adaptation Builds Complexity*, Reading, Massachusetts: Addison-Wesley Publishing Co, 1995.

Holloway, John and Eloina Pelaez ed, *Zapatista! Reinventing Revolution in Mexico*, London: Pluto Press, 1998.

Johnston, Robert W. *The Resiliency of Terrorist Havens: A Social Mobilization Theory Approach.* Masters Thesis, Naval Post Graduate School, 2006.

Jomini, Antoine H. *The Art of War.* In *Roots of Strategy: Book 2.* Harrison, PA: Stackpole Books, 1987.

Joint Chiefs of Staff, *Joint Publication 1-02, Department of Defense Dictionary of Military and Associated Terms*, 12 April, 2001 (As amended through 4 Mar, 2008).

Joint Chiefs of Staff, *Joint Publication 2-01.3 Joint Tactics, Techniques and Procedures for Joint Intelligence Preparation of the Battlespace*, 24 May 2000.

Joint Chiefs of Staff, *Joint Publication 3-0, Joint Operations*, 17 September 2006

Joint Chiefs of Staff, *Joint Publication 5-0, Joint Operation Planning*, 26 December 2006

Kepel, Gilles. *The War for Muslim Minds.* Cambridge, Massachusetts: The Belknap Press of Harvard University Press, 2004.

Leahy, Kevin C. *The Impact of Technology on the Command, Control, and Organizational Structure of Insurgent Groups.* Ft Leavenworth, KS: Command and General Staff College, 2005.

Macdonald, Douglas J. *The New Totalitarians: Social Identities and Radical Islamist Political Grand Strategy.* Carlisle, PA: Strategic Studies Institute (SSI), 2007.

MIPT Terrorism Knowledge Base legal case profile 00-CR-147. 10 September 2007 <http://www.tkb.org/CaseHome.jsp?caseid=615>. [09/27, 2007].

Naveh, Shimon, *In Pursuit of Military Excellence: The Evolution of Operational Theory*, Portland, OR: Frank Cass Publishers, 1997.

Paget, Julian, *Counter-Insurgency Warfare: Techniques of Guerilla Warfare*, New York, NY: Walker and Company, 1967.

Paret, Peter, ed. *Makers of Modern Strategy: from Machiavelli to the Nuclear Age*, Princeton, NJ: Princeton University Press, 1986.

Rabasa, Angel et al., *TheGlobal Jihadist Movement, Santa Monica*, CA: RAND, 2006.

LTC William T. Sorrells et al., *Systemic Operational Design: An Introduction*, Fort Leavenworth, KS: United States Army Command and General Staff College School of Advanced Military Studies, 2005.

Taber, Robert, *War of the Flea: the Classic Study of Guerrilla Warfare*, Washington D.C: Brassey's Inc, 2002.

Thomas, Timothy L. *Cyber silhouettes: Shadows over information operations.* Fort Leavenworth, KS: Foreign Military Studies Office, 2005.

Tone, John L. *The Fatal Knot: The Guerilla War in Navarre and the Defeat of Napoleon in Spain.* Chapel Hill: The University of North Carolina Press, 1994.

Tuathail, Geroid O., "De-Territorialised Threats and Global Dangers: Geopolitics and Risk Society," *Boundaries, Territory, and Postmodernity*, ed. David Newman, Portland, OR: F. Cass, 1999, 17-29.

Turabian, Kate L. *A Manual for Writers of Research Papers, Theses, and Dissertations.* 7th ed. Chicago: University of Chicago Press, 2007.

U.S. Army. *FM 3-24 Counterinsurgency*, December, 2006.

U.S. Army. *TRADOC Pamphlet 525-FW-X, Commanders Appreciation and Campaign Design*, Version 3.0, Fort Monroe: HQ US Army Training and Doctrine Command, 2007.